Prayers to ᵣ....

*An introduction
and selection of prayers, with exercises,
for group or personal use.*

Graham Pigott

Vicar of St. Paul's, Wilford Hill, Nottingham

GROVE BOOKS LIMITED
BRAMCOTE NOTTINGHAM NG9 3DS

Contents

The twelve prayers may be photocopied for use in small groups within local churches.
For enquiries about wider use, please contact the publishers.

Acknowledgements

I am appreciative of the encouragement of Canon Ian Bunting to develop both this form of booklet and this area of pastoral concern, and to Mrs. Elizabeth Snodgrass for help with word processing! I am also very grateful to all those at St. Paul's Wilford Hill and in experimental spirituality groups who have encouraged me to explore and discover ways of helping people to pray through sharing with me their own experiences of praying their way through life.

The **Cover Illustration** is by kind permission of
A.P. Westerbook Ltd. (publishers of religious cards),
19 Sackville Road, Bexhill-on-Sea, East Sussex, England, TN39 3JH.

First Impression February1995
ISSN 0262-799X
ISBN 1 85174 285 9

1
Down Memory Lane

'Forgetfulness is the root of all evil.'[1]

What prayers do you remember from childhood? Many? Few? None? For me it is only the Lord's Prayer, in the traditional version, learnt through reciting it daily in school assembly. I also learnt a few verses from the hymns we sang, in particular *All things bright and beautiful*. I did not learn by heart any other prayers which I can recite from memory until I became an Anglican in my thirties. However I was encouraged to memorise Scripture as a youngster in Bible class, the first verses being Proverbs 3.5 and 6:

> Trust in the Lord with all thine heart;
> and lean not unto thine own understanding.
> In all thy ways acknowledge him
> and he shall direct thy paths.

Later, in my late teens, I began learning verses such as Psalm 119.11 and 105:

> Thy word have I hid in mine heart
> that I might not sin against thee;

and

> Thy word is a lamp unto my feet,
> and a light unto my path.

I remember too, listening in assembly at grammar school to the fascinating rhythm of Philippians 4.8 being read with all its repeated 'whatsoevers'...

> whatsoever things are true,
> whatsoever things are honest,
> whatsoever things are just,
> whatsoever things are pure,
> whatsoever things are lovely,
> whatsoever things are of good report:
> if there be any virtue, and if there be any praise,
> think on these things.

But no prayers struck me or were repeated often enough for me to notice or

---

1 An unknown Egyptian monk

begin to learn and remember them for myself.

Growing up completely outside the Anglican tradition, and largely outside the Christian church for many years, I had very little opportunity to develop a Christian memory. What I did acquire along the way were verses of hymns and scriptures rather than prayers. The evangelical tradition I was influenced by considered written prayers and liturgy an anathema! All prayer was to be extempore, invented in the moment, spoken from the heart. But I found this to be an impossible ideal and a burdensome expectation. It is not in the spirit of Scripture which includes the book of psalms as a prayer book within the Bible, and has had a central place in both Jewish and Christian worship and personal spirituality, encouraging the memorising of passages.

I soon realised that the long, meandering, extemporary prayers that I was hearing were full of favourite phrases, which others sometimes repeated, creating oral liturgies peppered with the word 'just' or adopting phraseology that was idiosyncratic if not very unhelpful. An example is the description of those who were ill as 'those who are laid on one side on a bed of sickness'.

As I began to be invited to lead services I also began to search for resources, selecting sections of the psalms and from books of prayers which I felt I could use to lead prayers in public and also expressed what I desired to say. This stretched me into new thinking and praying beyond my personal limitations. In the 1960s William Barclay was writing prolifically. His *Prayers for the Christian Year* became one of my favourite resources, introducing me to liturgical structures, rhythms and forms, which I have valued ever since.[2] Even so, I was still not experiencing the corporate solidarity of common prayer and the enormous value of a Christian community sharing a common resource of prayer for both personal and public use. That came years later. When we recite together the same words of prayer in worship, we begin to have within us a common memory for personal prayer during the week and a common memory as a Christian community.

I really began to appreciate this when I became an Anglican in the mid-1970s, during a period of difficult spiritual dryness. Two significant things were happening. First, my ability to pray extemporarily and conversationally dried up almost completely. I recognised that I had a growing need for written prayers to help me in personal prayer and when sharing in public worship. By then I was attending an Anglican church using the Series 3 Holy Communion service, the forerunner to ASB Rite A. This had become my mainstay, especially the Kyries and the Collect for Purity. Then I found an earlier version of this collect at the beginning of *The Cloud of Unknowing* and it became my only daily prayer for weeks, with unusually helpful effects:

---

2   William Barclay *Prayers for the Christian Year* (SCM, London, date unknown)

God
unto whom all hearts are open
unto whom all wills do speak,
from whom no secret thing is hidden,
I beseech thee
so to cleanse the purpose of my heart
with the unutterable gift of thy grace
that I may perfectly love thee,
and worthily praise thee. Amen[3]

The alternative words were stunning, and in typing them again nearly twenty years later, they speak to me with greater depth than the familiar words that I love and recite regularly:

Almighty God,
to whom all hearts are open,
all desires known,
and from whom no secrets are hidden:
cleanse the thoughts of our hearts
by the inspiration of your Holy Spirit,
that we may perfectly love you
and worthily magnify your holy name,
through Jesus Christ our Lord. Amen[4]

During those dry weeks and months, this prayer was the only prayer I prayed, daily, slowly, in a short period of quiet, before I went to work. The effect I have often likened to the simmering process in jam making when the heat is critical, the jam is forming, and the bits come to the surface and need to be carefully skimmed off each time they rise. And that is how this prayer worked in my life as the Holy Spirit did his hidden work within, as I slowly recited the words each day. My scum came to the surface for me to acknowledge and then let go of, to God, and discover, as the older words say so beautifully *the unutterable gift of thy grace.*

I was being given a language through which I could articulate and co-operate with the Spirit's work within me, words tested by years of common usage, reminding me that in my desert searching and seeming solitude I was sharing in a constant stream and heritage of prayer stretching over hundreds of years into the gift of the present moment. A single prayer, written by an unknown author, so many years ago, gradually learned by heart,

3 Author unknown. Translation and introduction by Clifton Walters *The Cloud of Unknowing* (Harmondsworth, Middlesex, 1961) p 42.
4 Holy Communion Rite A *Alternative Services Book* p 119.

5

became my gateway into God's presence and his inner cleansing.

After a while I discovered the prayer of the Grail Community (based in Pinner, Middlesex) and added this as a prayer of self-offering daily before I left home for work:[5]

> Lord Jesus,
>> I give you my hands
>>> to do your work.
>> I give you my feet
>>> to go your way.
>> I give you my eyes
>>> to see as you do.
>> I give you my tongue
>>> to speak your words.
>> I give you my mind
>>> that you may think in me.
>> I give you my spirit
>>> that you may pray in me.
>> Above all, I give you my heart
>>> that you may love in me your Father
>>> and all mankind.
>> I give you my whole self
>>> that you may grow in me,
>> so that it is you, Lord Jesus,
>>> who live and work and pray in me. Amen.

What I still appreciate about this prayer is the practical consecration combined with a desire to be prayed in and so become a self through whom God can express himself. That insight revolutionised my understanding of Christian prayer and living.

My second significant experience during that time was a struggle with the intimidations of spiritual darkness, in a way that is hard to describe. The 1970s were years when a renewed interest in the occult was developing. We were having unpleasant disturbances in the house, which affected our children. So I sought help and was introduced to some of the prayers in the service of Compline. Peace returned, we slept better and the disturbances ended as my wife and I learnt to recite this collect frequently at night:

> Visit this house, we pray you, Lord;
>> Drive far from it the snares of the enemy;
> May your holy angels dwell with us
>> and guard us in peace;

And may your blessing be always upon us;
through Jesus Christ our Lord. Amen.

Out of this experience we helped our young children to learn the evening collect, *Lighten our darkness*, by heart so that we could say it together at bedtime, along with others from a favourite book of prayers or our own words. Another prayer which I value knowing by heart and have included in the twelve prayers to explore towards the end of the booklet, is the simple, yet exquisitely apt, antiphon that accompanies the *Nunc Dimittis* in Compline:

Save us, Lord, while we are awake;
guard us while we are asleep;
that awake we may watch with Christ,
and asleep may rest in his peace.

The economy of words, the balancing of being awake or sleeping, and the appropriate petitions for each condition are so complete, whether asking for help and attentive consciousness when awake or protection and the healing rest of sleep. This is my favourite prayer if I find myself awake in the small hours of the night and unable to return to sleep. Then lying awake for a while can take on a new role akin to the psalmist who meditated in the watches of the night (Psalm 63.6) and waited for the morning (Psalm 130.6). Later on, I valued using Bishop George Appleton's popular compilation *Daily Prayer and Praise*, which provides morning and evening prayers for a month, and includes some prayers which he wrote himself. One which I have returned to frequently and used in services of healing and meditation is a prayer to the Holy Spirit:

O Spirit of God,
who dost speak to spirits
created in thine own likeness,
Penetrate into the depth of our spirits
into the storehouse of memories
remembered and forgotten,
into the depths of being,
the very springs of personality
And cleanse and forgive, making us whole and holy
That we may be thine,
and live in the new being
of Christ our Lord.[5]

5   George Appleton *Daily Prayer and Praise* (Lutterworth Press, London, 1962) Day 15, Evening Prayer, no 156.

I have resisted the temptation to iron out the traditional turn of phrase, which can easily be done to adapt it to 'ASB' English, so that you can appreciate it as I discovered it and first used it. Often the older turn of phrase can contain a richness and convey a greater sense of the mystery of God for some people, and we can retain this if it helps us when praying on our own. Some prayers, I think, resist all attempts to adapt them. A favourite which illustrates this is the 13th century *Veni Sancti Spiritus* (Come Holy Spirit):

> What is soilèd make thou pure;
> What is wounded work its cure;
> What is parched fructify;
> What is rigid gently bend;
> What is frozen warmly tend;
> Strengthen what goes erringly.

The very strangeness of the language of each petition invites me to ponder words which I would not normally use, yet capture the essential healing work of the Holy Spirit, who is at the heart of prayer, whether read, written, said or sung, our words or another's.

Neither this personal trip down memory lane nor this booklet are intended to suggest one way of praying is superior to another, or even essential for everybody. I survive the varied work demands of most days on short arrow prayers of thanksgiving, praise and petition, or meditating briefly on a few lines or phrases from a prayer, hymn, or Scripture. But I do value time in each day to sit and read an office or prayers written by others. These can stretch me beyond myself into the greater vision and spirituality of the whole church, feeding and renewing my Christian memory. Recently I have used the alternative collects and prayers written by Janet Morley. Her use of language invites me to renew the 'yes' of my mind and appreciate new ways of recognising how God is present and seeking to work in us and all his creation. I find she uses words skilfully to express perceptive Christian insights:

> Christ our companion,
> you came not to humiliate the sinner
> but to disturb the righteous.
> Welcome us when we are put to shame,
> but challenge our smugness,
> that we may truly turn from what is evil,
> and be freed even from our virtues,
> in your name, Amen.[6]

---

6 Janet Morley *All Desires Known* (SPCK, London, 1992) p 10.

We live at a time when we have good access to a wonderful heritage of Christian prayers, old and new, which can enrich and shape our own praying. I am indebted to that great inheritance. I could wish that I had been introduced earlier and learned more of them so that I could remember and recite more by heart. But I came to this heritage later, by a different route, and I value what I have discovered. Some I have included here. Others are in the selection for group or personal reflection. I hope you will be encouraged to discover, explore, learn, meditate and share through using prayers that can deepen your relating to God in all his grace and mystery.

A Suggested Exercise:

Sit quietly and make a list of any lines of prayers that you have found helpful in your Christian pilgrimage. Then tick those which you think you can remember by heart.

2
Well-Chosen Words

A little can go a long way. A few words, well chosen, apt for the situation, can be far more effective than too many. I was reminded of this during the final session of a recent parish weekend. The guest leader, skilled in adult Christian education, had spoken for less than an hour during a total of over six hours of sessions of learning together. He had enabled us to explore and share together, and make some very important and personal discoveries of God in our own experience. In our final session we were expressing our appreciation, and one person thanked him for *well-chosen words*. I have remembered that appreciative phrase, so accurate and concisely expressed, identifying a key element that had helped to make the parish weekend such a valuable and refreshing time spiritually.

Our ideas about prayer are often influenced by the sort of prayers we hear in church and the way we hear others pray. The great prayers of our Christian heritage are often expressed through the economy of well chosen words, crafted in the presence of God. That process is prayer itself, a searching for the right words and phrasing to express the desire of the writer and in so doing embodying key elements of the way in which they knew and trusted in God in their own experience.

Metropolitan Anthony reminds us that

'Forms of speech, methods of expression, will change with the semantics of a language, with the epoch in which they are spoken, with the contexts in which they are used...until you come to formulations of a few words which contain—as in a nutshell—a kernel that is so tiny, dry and compact, yet holds *life* within itself, and which, if you will let it take root in you, will begin to disclose to you a vision of life that will enable you to grow into what you are called to be.'[7]

The great prayers of our Christian heritage are often like this. Sometimes they are couched in the language of a different age, spiritual culture or tradition, yet contain an essence which can come to life in our hearts and minds as we ponder them and pray them. Others are deceptively simple, economic with words, yet pregnant with meaning, translating easily into our own age.

An accessible prayer which invites this kind of engagement is the honed words of Sir Thomas More. I imagine him waiting, imprisoned in the Tower of London, with time on his hands and his future in the balance, shut away from his friends and family and the comforts of his home, stripped of high office and facing the probability of execution. He prayed and wrote:

> Thank you, dear Jesus,
> for all that you have given me,
> for all that you have taken from me,
> for all you have left me.

A prayer like this invites meditation, probes personal experience, suggests a new way of evaluating what has happened to us in our journey through life up to the present moment. I have given this prayer on a card to many people in different pastoral situations, including those of bereavement and illness. Recently in a small service, a woman who is living courageously and creatively with cancer following surgery made this her prayer, saying it aloud. I was deeply moved, knowing her story, and realised afresh that these words were no longer those of Sir Thomas More only, inscribed with calligraphic skill as a prayer card, as illustrated on the front cover, but the well chosen words that now conveyed her struggle and letting go, out of which has come deep spiritual and personal growth. A little can go a long way, and enable us to pray with a new clarity from deep within ourselves.

A Suggested Exercise:

Make a list of the phrases from the liturgy or from prayers that you appreciate which are like 'well-chosen words' for you, encapsulating what you believe or desire as a Christian.

---

7   Anthony Bloom, Metropolitan of Sourozh *God and Man* (Hodder, London, 1974) p 56.

3
A Christian Knapsack?

Two things are happening at present which can affect what we store in our Christian memory. First, our liturgies are changing, not just from BCP to ASB, but in the growth of seasonal material, such as *The Promise of His Glory*,[8] and of alternatives for use within a basic Anglican framework, as in *A Service of the Word and Affirmations of Faith*.[9] Secondly, we are being made aware of other alternatives outside the usual English Anglican liturgies, such as the worship and prayer resources from the Wild Goose Fellowship based at Iona, off the west coast of Scotland, and the Taizé community in France. Whilst all this is enriching and stimulating, it also means we are using a greater variety of material, repeated less frequently, and therefore remembered less easily, unless a deliberate effort is made to learn some of the prayers.

Concern is now being expressed about the difficulty in this situation for people to acquire or retain a core of common prayers with which they are familiar, even if these are not known well enough to recite without a printed format to hand. Of course, letting go of printed prompts might motivate more of us to learn the liturgical prayers and responses that we use and so be able to recite them. We are privileged to have the reprographic technology, service books or leaflets and finance in most cases to reproduce the words we use in worship. Yet it is these very facilities that lead to alternatives becoming increasingly available, and thereby contributing to the demise of some aspects of the traditional concept of common prayer.

The Latin tag *lex orandi, lex credendi*, meaning what is spoken in prayer is what is believed, is fundamental to Anglican liturgy and spirituality. The spoken word both expresses and frames the understanding of Christian faith. So the liturgy and additional prayers are of central significance in the passing on of Christian faith, both within and between generations. Bishop Michael Ramsey believed that the Anglican way of introducing some people to Christian faith was to say 'Come and pray with us', for to experience the prayers and worship was to come to know the way Anglicans believe.

Revd Michael Vasey, of the Liturgical Commission of the Church of England, has emphasised how 'familiar patterns and texts play an important part in structuring and deepening the discipleship of individual Christians'.[10]

---

8   The Liturgical Commission of the General Synod of the Church of England, *The Promise of His Glory* (Church House Publishing and Mowbrays, London, 1991).
9   The Liturgical Commission, *A Service of the Word and Affirmations of Faith* (Church House Publishing, London, 1994)
10 Michael Vasey, 'Sustaining the Core of Worship', in the *Church Times*, 25th June 1993, an abridged extract from Michael Perham (ed) *The Renewal of Common Prayer* (1993).

His observation appreciates how important is the interaction between corporate worship and personal prayer. Canon Alan Wilkinson recognised this in calling for an Anglican knapsack of prayers on which individuals could draw in a crisis.[11] We can develop this idea by thinking of our lives as a pilgrimage. Then ask, what prayers would I like to have as a resource for my life journey? The image can be stretched to think of these prayers as a first aid kit for times of crisis, or clothing for winter storms or different seasons of the spirit, available to us through knowing them well enough to be able to recite them.

Whilst some of this core collection of prayers would be in the current liturgies of the Church of England, others would not, having been discovered from different sources. What prayers would these be? Do they easily select themselves or is our heritage so great that choosing an essential few to create this core would prove exceedingly difficult? These are key questions for Anglicans as we respond to new developments in liturgy and worship as well as use a variety of other resources for personal prayer.

When discussing this booklet in a Grove committee, we did not find that we could agree on a core twelve. We were nowhere near unanimous, revealing the large number of prayers from which a choice can be made. The final selection of prayers on the loose-leaf sheets for you to explore and consider learning so as to remember, is mine. Choosing them has been like the challenge of selecting my desert island discs! They include some of my favourites which have nourished me. I have deliberately omitted the Lord's Prayer because of its unique significance as the prayer given by Jesus.

One practical point which I considered carefully was whether the prayer texts for you to explore should be in the same type face and approximate size or in calligraphy, which I enjoy personally or mentally, trying different possibilities. Expressive calligraphy would prevent such initial neutrality, and not leave the reader responsible for their own consciousness. Some of the exercises will suggest ways to develop this.

Suggested Activities:

What prayers would you like to be able to remember for life? Other ways of considering this are to ask yourself:

What prayers would I like everyone to know?

What prayers would I want to pass on to the next generation?

Make your own scrap-book of prayers. This can be a worthwhile venture, collecting prayer cards, copying from books or service sheets, sorting them into your own order and groupings for personal use.

11 'Opinion' in the *Church Times*, 1st May 1992.

4
Read, Mark, Learn, and Inwardly Digest!

I learnt this saying at school before ever I knew where it came from. It was one of my teacher's favourite instructions when exhorting us to work in class. I was pleasantly surprised, years later, to find these words in the collect for 2nd Sunday in Advent, in both the Book of Common Prayer and the ASB. The selection of twelve prayers on the loose leaf sheets is to help you to do just that, suggesting ways you can explore and pray them. Here I will outline briefly some of the basic ways in which we can helpfully use prayers written by other Christians.

Basically we learn what to say by learning how to say it, whether we are copying someone else, experimenting and being corrected, or reading someone else's words. We internalise language in the same way. Have you ever heard yourself thinking or saying aloud phrases of your parents or local idioms? Ready-made prayers, provided they are related to our stage of development, can help us to grow into other ways of expressing ourselves and also inherit our spiritual tradition. They can help us to appreciate rhythm, forms of words, thoughts about God or verbal images, the aim always being to help us reach through the words to the living reality of God.

Simon Tugwell believes that the very recalcitrance of the words is a sacramental means by which the transcendence of God is made present to us.[12] There is a connection between mediation and meditation. God comes to us through the materiality of things, including words and images. We use these to express our understanding of God and our desire to communicate with God. So when we use written prayers we are seeking to listen as well as speak through the words, desiring to encounter the reality of God's presence. Therefore we will have a different aim in our reading.

Most of us scan read much of the time, aiming to gain an overall understanding as we move quickly through a page and on to the next. We tend to read even personal correspondence this way too. This can be a subtle way of being disrespectful when we consider the different length of time it takes to write a personal letter than to read it. That difference of time is about the effort invested by the writer to share their news and thoughts, compared to the receptivity of the reader to them. To receive in any way that is to have value we need to give time, to change pace, to slow down, to consider the words more carefully and let ourselves be involved in them. Love letters are read many times, the reader savouring the meanings between the lines! Slow repetition is the basic requirement, enabling a gradual absorption of the

12 Simon Tugwell *Prayer. Volume 1: Living with God* (Veritas Publications, Dublin, 1974) p 9.

words. This may well lead to memorising them, sensing the phrasing and structure, noting the particularity of the language, letting it resonate more deeply within. *Lectio divina*, or divine reading, is the traditional way of praying written texts. It has four aspects:

Lectio divina: read slowly, even repeating the words under your breath or aloud.

Meditatio: ruminate deeply, rather like a cow chewing the cud, or a child sucking a boiled sweet, enjoying the taste, without analysing. The purpose of this process is to help the words descend from mind to the heart.

Oratio: respond honestly, conversing with God as a friend.

Contemplatio: rest deeply, relaxing into God and receiving from God.

Always be ready to digress into persistent personal concerns as they are stirred in response to the words and images in the text and weave them into prayerful meditation, seeking to discern which are simply distractions to let go of. Then return to the written prayer. In many ways the text of the prayer is there as a runaway to help you take off into the presence of God, or to use the image in reverse, help you to descend slowly and land safely, grounded in God. God is not taken in by our polite little speeches, nor our accurate recitations.[13] He is listening to our hearts…and speaking in our hearts. The written texts can be the medium of this encounter, and I pray they will become so for you. And when they do not seem to be that, they can still be an expression, through our will to say them, of the desires we desire, yet do not currently feel. God is still at work through his Spirit within us.

A Suggested Exercise:

Make a list of the possible advantages and disadvantages of being able to recite prayers by heart. How do they offset each other?

---

13 Tugwell *op cit* p 11.

5
Pastoral Value

The pastoral value of knowing well crafted prayers by heart becomes clearer as soon as we consider pastoral care. Some people may have failing sight or blindness, leading them to develop and depend on their capacity to remember. Others may lose their capacity to hold a book or even turn a page. Yet others may be deeply troubled within and find the resource of remembered prayers an encouragement and defence against some of their thoughts or recurrent moods, or problems with concentration. In the week I was writing this section, I recited prayers on two different occasions with people I was seeking to help, and they valued joining in with me. We were bonded through common prayer. One said how in times of stress—for her husband had been taken into hospital—she relied on recalling familiar prayers learnt by heart. Repeating them was all she could cope with in her anxiety.

I have already begun to illustrate the pastoral value of prayer cards. Many people's everyday spirituality is at this level. For some it is their sole source of prayers and I have been amazed to discover how the simple gift of a prayer on a card can be greatly valued, particularly when journeying through illness or grief. Two or three prayer cards beside the bed may be as much as a person in sickness or suffering can manage. They can be a significant source of comfort in the long hours of darkness at night. Years later I have been shown a discoloured bent card that has been treasured and has been a way of praying when lost for words or all prayer had dried up. I know of parishioners who carry them in their handbags or wallets, look at them in bus or train, absorbing their truth and praying the words.

I was once shown a card of the great prayer of St. Ignatius, *Lord, teach me to be generous, to give and not to count the cost...* It had been carried by a husband in his wallet ever since he was given it by a padre in the Second World War. It was dated and repaired with sellotape. Yet the man had never spoken of his faith or ever went to church. His wife discovered it after his death.

Other cards I have seen propped up on the mantle piece, pinned on a kitchen notice board, blue-tacked to a wall, half tucked behind a calendar or picture. They are ever in danger of being unnoticed as part of the furniture, yet witness to a significant moment or time when they were read, valued, and said what was hard to articulate oneself. The prayers of others give us words to say, enabling us to express what we find inexpressible.

I have found two very comprehensive sources that I use and can recommend for buying in any quantity. Both suppliers will send catalogues and price lists on request.

They are:

A.P. Westerbrook,
19 Sackville Road,
Bexhill-on-Sea,
East Sussex,
TN39 3JH

(a sample is on the front cover, by permission).

Tim Tiley Prints,
Eblana Lodge,
157 Cheltenham Road,
Bristol,
BS6 5RR

Most of their prayer cards are in traditional language. I have yet to discover a printer using modern English versions. Smaller quantities and individual cards are often available in cathedrals, Christian bookshops and some churches. If your church does not offer this facility, it is well worth considering starting it because of the value pastorally and in encouraging spiritual development. You would be providing a simple way of feeding these areas of personal need.

Suggested exercises:
    Make a collection of prayer cards for pastoral use and consider in what situations each might be appropriately given.
    Ask other Christians (or people you know well enough to ask) if they have ever appreciated receiving a prayer card or knowing a prayer well enough to recite it, and what was the particular occasion when they valued this.

1. **Almighty God,**
    to whom all hearts are open,
    all desires known,
    and from whom no secrets are hidden:
    cleanse the thoughts of our hearts
    by the inspiration of your Holy Spirit,
    that we may perfectly love you,
    and worthily magnify your name;
    through Jesus Christ our Lord.

The Collect for Purity (ASB. p.119)

This is the prayer at the beginning of the communion service in both the Book of Common Prayer 1662 and the Alternative Services Book 1980 with only minor changes. An older version was included in the first chapter of this booklet.

Ways to explore this prayer (with suggested times for each stage):
1. Read the prayer slowly and silently several times, seeing which words or phrases draw your attention. Note these by underlining or marking them in some way. *(5 minutes)*
    You may like to try the more personal form using 'I' and 'me'.

2. Now give time to repeating these words or phrases slowly. Perhaps you will come to favour just one or two. *(10 minutes)*

3. Reflect on the thoughts and feelings that you experienced whilst doing this, and listen for how you seemed to be aware of God in the quiet and through being with this prayer. Note any distractions or areas of struggling too. Then ask:

    What is the Holy Spirit prompting and bringing to your consciousness? How do you want to respond? *(10 minutes, perhaps noting any thoughts)*

4. Say the prayer together, slowly, then take turns in the group to say your most significant phrase, without comment, pausing between each, noting both the variety and similarity of choice.

5. Divide into twos or threes to share something of what you experienced in praying the prayer this way, listening to each other in turn, without discussing. *(10 minutes)*

6. Finally come together to say the prayer together again.

Prayer One

2.   **Almighty God,**
     you have made us for yourself,
     and our hearts are restless
     till they find their rest in you.
     Teach us to offer ourselves to your service,
     that here we may have your peace,
     and in the world to come may see you face to face;
     through Jesus Christ our Lord
                              The Collect for Pentecost 18 (ASB p. 722)

This prayer expresses a conviction of St. Augustine of Hippo, Bishop in North Africa (354-430 AD). He was aware of a restlessness that is related to seeking God, and declines only as you come to trust his grace and rest in his peace?

Ways to explore this prayer (with suggested times):

1. Begin by reading the prayer together three times, pausing between each.

2. Then reflect on the day , or perhaps the past fews days, noting when you have been most restless and most at peace.   *(5 minutes)*

3. Pray for light to see yourself more clearly. Then explore the following questions:
a) Can you discern what triggered your times of restlessness and greater peace?
b) Was the source something outside you or something within you?
c) What does this tell you about yourself?   *(10 minutes)*

4. Try to imagine the face of God, as revealed in Jesus Christ (2 Corinthians 4.7). What qualities and kind of presence are you aware of?   *(5 minutes)*

5. Now let your insights become personal prayers, perhaps of confession, or desire for help or healing, finishing with self -offering.   *(10 minutes)*

6. Consider what you would like to share from this experience. Then do so in twos or threes, listening respectfully to each other in turn.
                              (10-15 minutes)

7. Finish by two people reading the prayer aloud with a pause in between, and finally reading the prayer together.

Prayer Two

3.   **Eternal God,**
the light of the minds that know you,
the joy of the wills that serve you;
grant us so to know you
that we may truly love you,
and so to love you
that we may fully serve you,
whom to serve is perfect freedom,
in Jesus Christ our Lord.

After St. Augustine (354-430 AD)

Ways to use this prayer (with suggested times):
Have a lighted candle in the centre to symbolise God both as the one who is light and gives light, and your shared search for light in the sense of Christian vision.

1. Begin by sitting quietly with the first three lines of the prayer and the lighted candle letting thoughts and images come and go until you seem to come to settle with one. *(5 minutes)*

2. Write your main thought(s) and / or draw a simple picture of the image which comes to you on a sheet of paper, and note the main feeling you were aware of whilst doing this. *(5 minutes)*

3. When everyone is ready, show them to each other without commenting. (You could lay them in a circle around the candle or hold them up in front of you). Then take turns, if you wish, to describe your own in a few descriptive sentences and share your main feeling, listening to the similarities and differences among you stirred by the same three lines of prayer!

4. Then read the prayer through together, aloud. Notice the developing movement in the prayer:
knowing, truly loving, fully serving, perfect freedom.

5. Now return to the fourth and fifth lines. Read this couplet silently a few times, asking, What knowledge of God might help me / us to love God more, and move towards willing service and greater freedom?
(5 minutes)
Then share your thoughts.

6. Finally, listen to the prayer being read once, and after a brief silence read it together.

Prayer Three

4.   **Grant, Lord,**
      that we may hold to you without parting,
      worship you without wearying,
      serve you without failing;
      faithfully seek you,
      happily find you,
      and forever possess you,
      the only God,
      blessed, now and for ever.

St. Anselm of Canterbury (1033-1109)

Anselm was a monk and prior, a gifted philosopher and theologian, an archbishop and reformer, and a person of prayer.

Ways to explore this prayer (with suggested times):
    This ancient prayer has a very simple introductory address, followed by two triple phrases focussed on God, as the Lord and only God, who is utterly desirable and worthy of complete devotion ('you' is repeated six times!).

1. Begin by reflecting on how you prefer to address God. Do you have a favourite title or name? Print two of them on a sheet of paper in large letters and place them around the lighted candle.   *(5 minutes)*

2. Discuss the strengths and weaknesses of using the title Lord.
                                                              (10 minutes)
3. Reflect prayerfully on the first triplet of requests. How are you aware of parting, wearying, or failing, the Lord? Then use your insights to write a short prayer of personal confession.
                                                              (10 minutes)
4. Share in twos or threes, and if you wish, read your prayer, listening to each other in turn, with respect, and saying a short sentence which affirms God's forgiveness.

5. Now consider the moods expressed in the second triplet of phrases. Note down the feelings that come to mind as you repeat these lines to yourself including the final words of praise to God.
                                                              (5 minutes)

    Then share briefly in twos or threes.

6. Finally, what do you desire the Lord God to grant you now? Ask him! Silently or aloud in the group. Then close by reading the complete prayer together.

Prayer Four

5.   Lord Jesus Christ, we thank you,
      for all the benefits you have won for us,
      for all the pains and insults you have borne for us.
      Most merciful redeemer,
      friend and brother,
      may we know you more clearly,
      love you more dearly,
      and follow you more nearly,
      day by day.

                                St. Richard of Chichester (1197-1253)

The traditional version begins: 'Thanks be to Thee, my Lord Jesus Christ, for all…' The version chosen here is from the ASB Confirmation Service (p. 259) and has been turned into the plural for corporate use in public worship.

Ways to explore this prayer (with suggested times):
You may find help in having one or more crucifixes or pictures of the crucifixion on display for the group to look at. If you are able to find ones that come from different parts of the world this will highlight the contrasts. (You could ask the group members to bring one.) Display these on a low table or on a board for all to see.

1. Begin by reading the prayer together. Then read the prayer to yourself in the more personal form, using 'I' and 'me'.

2. Draw a large cross on a piece of paper. Using different coloured pens list above the crossbeam - the benefits, and below the crossbeam - the pains and insults, which you consider that the Lord Jesus Christ has won or borne for you. Meditating on the pictures or prayer may help you. How does this reveal Jesus as merciful redeemer, friend and brother to you?
                                                        (10 minutes)

3. Share your reflections in groups of three, noting what you have listed in common and what you had forgotten or not considered or realised before.
                                                        (15 minutes)

4. How have you been stirred as you meditated on what Jesus has done for you and who he desires to be to you? Reflect on your thoughts and feelings. How are you moved to respond? Use either the words of the prayer or your own.   *(5 minutes)*

5. Close by saying the prayer together.

                          Prayer Five

6. **Thank you, dear Jesus,**
   for all you have given me,
   for all you have taken away from me,
   for all you have left me.

St. Thomas More (c.1478-1535)

Sir Thomas More was a scholar and moral theologian, Chancellor of all England for Henry VIII, then martyr, beheaded for refusing to sign an oath that acknowleded supreme allegiance to the king, when as a Roman Catholic, his first and greater allegiance was to the Pope.

A way to explore praying this prayer (with suggested times):

1. Read this prayer through slowly a few times, then meditate quietly noting down your reflections on a sheet of paper divided into three sections headed:

   Given me   Taken away from me   Left me

   (Allow 10 or 15 minutes)

2. Then if you feel able, being sensitive to your own sense of gratitude or distress, for grief may be felt in recalling losses, pray this prayer silently, adding in after each of the three key lines some or all of your own lists as you feel able. Remember to be gentle with yourself and not to force yourself to put into your prayer anything you are not ready to offer to God. The time may not be right. Rather, ask God for grace to be able to pray about that specific issue some day in the future.   *(5 minutes)*

3. Share together, in twos or threes, what you are willing to disclose from your lists, listening respectfully to each other, discovering what you have in common and how different our life experience can be.   *(15 minutes)*

4. Close with a time of prayer as a group, using your extended versions of this prayer if you feel able, knowing others will endorse your prayer with an 'Amen', or 'So let it be!' of supportive agreement.

5. To end, you could say the prayer together after a short silence, putting it into the plural 'us' form.

7.
> Christ be with me,
> Christ within me,
> Christ behind me,
> Christ before me,
> Christ beside me,
> Christ to win me,
> Christ to comfort
> and restore me.
> Christ beneath me,
> Christ above me,
> Christ in quiet,
> Christ in danger,
> Christ in hearts of
> all that love me,
> Christ in mouth of
> friend and stranger.

This is a verse from 'St. Patrick's Breastplate' (translated by Mrs. C.F. Alexander). St. Patrick (389-461 AD) was a monk and bishop, and a great missionary to the Irish. His emphasis on the priority of mission led to the evangelising of Europe by Celtic monks in the 6th and 7th centuries.

Ways to explore this prayer (with suggested times):
1. Begin by reading the prayer together once, then twice as a round, each person reading a couplet slowly, with pauses between them and a silence between the two readings.

2. Now read it quietly to yourself, noticing the Celtic love of rhythm and repetition and the affirmation of being surrounded by Christ and therefore protected on all sides. Try to imagine Christ in relation to yourself in all these different aspects in turn. *(10 minutes)*

3. In quiet, choose your favourite phrase or couplet. *(5 minutes)*

    Take turns in saying these aloud in the group. Which one is the most favoured? Were any omitted?

4. Consider which line is least true in your experience and for what possible reasons? You could ask Christ to help you to become aware of him in that way. *(5 minutes)*

5. Finish by saying the prayer together, using the plural 'us', instead of 'me'.

Prayer Seven

8.   **Lord Jesus,**
              I give you my hands
                  to do your work.
              I give you my feet
                  to go your way.
              I give you my eyes
                  to see as you do.
              I give you my tongue
                  to speak your words.
              I give you my mind
                  that you may think in me.
              I give you my spirit
                  that you may pray in me.
              Above all, I give you my heart
                  that you may love in me your Father
                  and all mankind.
              I give you my whole self
                  that you may grow in me,
              so that it is you, Lord Jesus
                  who live and work and pray in me.

The prayer of the Grail Community, Pinner, Middlesex.

Ways to explore this prayer (with suggested times):
1. This prayer can enable a practical and focussed self-offering. Begin by reading it through slowly and quietly to yourself, reflecting on each part that is mentioned. Consider how you have used them to express your life. How has the Lord Jesus been present, praying, living, loving and working through you?

    What ways of serving and self-offering have been more easy or natural for you?

    What ways have been difficult? Jot down some of your thoughts.
    (10 minutes)

2. Share some of your reflections in threes, including both something that you find comes naturally and something with which you struggle.
    (15 minutes)

3. Now consider what you are grateful for and what you regret. Then offer prayers of thanksgiving and confession, either silently or aloud as a group. Close by saying the prayer together changing it into the plural. (You may need to work out the changes together first!)

Prayer Eight

9.   **O Lord,**
           support us all the day long of this troublous life,
           until the shades lengthen and evening comes,
           and the busy world is hushed,
           the fever of life is over,
           and our work is done.
           Then, Lord, in your mercy
           grant us safe lodging, a holy rest,
           and peace at the last.
           through Jesus Christ our Lord.

after Cardinal John Henry Newman (1801-1890)

This prayer comes from a saying of Cardinal Newman which begins: 'May he support us…' As a prayer it has often been used towards the end of a day, though it is about the whole day as well. It is included as an optional prayer in the ASB funeral service, which is the version cited above. Its poetic imagery and rhythm can create a sense of coming to safety, rest and peace.

Ways to explore this prayer (with suggested times):
Have a lighted candle in the centre, symbolising the coming of the evening.

1. Begin with a period of quiet in which to settle and seek the presence of God. This can be helped by relaxing your body and letting your breathing slow down naturally.
   You may find it helpful to say 'O Lord' in rhythm with your breathing, seeking his presence as you breathe in, and letting out the worries and stresses of the day as you breathe out.   *(5 minutes)*

2. Now review the day so far. How has God been supporting you? Thank him for all that has been an encouragement, and share with him any disappointments and regrets.   *(10 minutes)*

3. Share as a group how this way of praying has helped you to let go of some of the busyness and fever of life and begin to sense God's peace?

4. Repeat and reflect on one or more of the three phrases: safe lodging, a holy rest, peace at the last.   *(10 minutes)*
   What thoughts, images and feelings were you aware of as you reflected? Share some of these in threes.   *(10 minutes)*

5. Finally, say the prayer together to close.

Prayer Nine

10. **Lighten our darkness,**
Lord we pray;
and in your mercy defend us
from all perils and dangers of this night;
for the love of your only Son,
our Saviour Jesus Christ.

Evening Prayer ASB

This prayer is also included in Compline. It has been set to music by the Revd. Chris Humphries, and is available in *The Late Evening Service* (Grove Worship Series Number 90)

Ways to explore this prayer (with suggested times):
Have a lighted candle in the centre to symbolise God as light in our darkness.

1. Begin by one person reading the prayer slowly, and after a silence in which to read it to yourself, read it again together.

2. Dim or switch off the lights and sit quietly, using the candle as a focus, and reflect on light in darkness. Lighten can mean lessen, lift or illuminate. What associations or feelings arise for you? What, for you, are the perils and dangers of the night? *(10 minutes)*

   Remember the words of the prologue of St. John's Gospel: 'The light shines in the darkness and the darkness has not understood or overcome it.' (John 1.5) And of Jesus: 'I am the light of the world.' (John 8.12).

3. Turn the lights on and share as a group some of your reflections, of light, darkness, perils and dangers, listening to each other with sensitivity and respect. *(15 minutes)*

4. Consider how appealing to the mercy of God might defend us? *(5 minutes)*

5. What help do you need to ask God for? Say the prayer silently using the singular 'I' and 'me', and include any special request for yourself arising out of your reflections. *(5 minutes)*

6. Finish by saying the prayer together.

Prayer Ten

11.   Watch Thou, dear Lord,
with those who wake, or watch or weep tonight;
and give thine angels charge over those who sleep.
Tend thy sick ones, O Lord.
Rest thy weary ones.
Bless thy dying ones.
Soothe thy suffering ones.
Pity thine afflicted ones.
And all for thy love's sake.

St. Augustine (354-430 AD)

In this prayer St. Augustine expresses the pastoral character of a vigil at the end of a full day of caring and serving when little more can be done for those in need than to appeal to Christ to help them.

Ways to explore this prayer (with suggested times):
Using a lighted candle may help to create a sense of waiting and watching in vigil.

1. Begin by imagining Jesus at prayer, first on the hills in the evening or at night, then being with people in need, looking, listening, touching, tending, speaking, caring, healing, blessing.   *(5 minutes)*

Remember that now he ever lives to intercede for us in the presence of God (Hebrews 7.25). So as you begin to pray, the *dear Lord* is already watching and praying, and angels are attending.

2. Think of those who may be lying awake, unable to sleep, those who watch in care or vigil, and those who weep in pity or compassion, or grief…with the sick, the weary, the dying, the suffering and the afflicted. You may wish to list the names of those who come to mind, grouping them under the different headings as in the prayer:
waking, watching, weeping, sick, weary (stressed), dying, suffering.
(10 minutes)

3. Now use the prayer to gather all the names in intercession. One person reads the prayer slowly, pausing each time one of the above groups is mentioned, so that you can speak out any of the names from your personal lists, appealing to the Lord's love.

4. Finish by having a short period of silence, and end by saying the prayer together.

Prayer Eleven

12.   **Save us, Lord, while we are awake,**
        guard us while we are asleep,
        that awake we may watch with Christ,
        and asleep we may rest in his peace.

The antiphon from Compline

This prayer is said as an antiphon preceding and following the reciting of the *Nunc Dimittis* (The Song of Simeon), acknowledging our vulnerability and need of help whether waking or sleeping, that in either state we may be with Christ.

Ways to explore this prayer (with suggested times):
A lighted candle as a focus can be a symbol of a night vigil, both our watching with Christ and our need for his saving presence as light.

1. Begin by saying the prayer together, slowly.

2. Then sit with the prayer, repeating it silently a few times, savouring its phrases. Sense which words are most significant for you.   *(5 minutes)*

3. Using colours pens and an A4 sheet of paper, write or print out the prayer using different size letters and colours to express the significance of the various words for you, adding any colouring or drawing if you wish. (You may want to do a quick rough to explore your ideas first.)
     (Allow 15 — 20 minutes)

4. Then share in twos what you have done, asking each other in turn what caused you to choose some of the colours and sizes of letters or words and their significance for you.   *(10 minutes)*

5. Arrange your illuminated prayers around the candle for all to see, and after a short period of quiet, say the prayer together twice to close, pausing in between.

Review:
You may, as a group, like to review your meditative exploring of these 12 prayers and share:
    a) what you have found helpful;
    b) which ones you can recite or intend to learn;
    c) any experience or insight that stands out for you.

Prayer Twelve